DEBORAH DERRICA DESIREE DESTINY
DIAHANN DIAMOND DIAN
DOROTHY EBELE EBONI EBONY EBONY JANICE
EDWIDGE EKERE EKHO ELAINE ELIZABETH
ELLAINE ELLEN ELSIE JEAN EMI ERICA
ESTHER EVIE ERYKAH EUGENIA FATIMAH
FELICE FREE GABRIELLE GISELLE GWENDOLYN
GRACE HADASSAH HALLE HARRIET HATTIE
HONEY IBO IDA IDRISSA IMANI INGENUE
IJEOMA IYEOKA JACQUELINE JADA JAHA
JAMILA JANET JASMYNE JAYNE JAZMIN
JENNAH JENNIFER JESMYN JESSICA JESSIE
JIMETTA JOAN JOHNNIE JONTERRI JORDIN

BLACK GIRL MAGIC

A POEM BY
**MAHOGANY
L. BROWNE**

ART BY *JESS X. SNOW*

Roaring Brook Press
New York

Text copyright © 2016 by Mahogany Browne
Illustrations copyright © 2016 by Jess X. Snow
Published by Roaring Brook Press
Roaring Brook Press is a division of Holtzbrinck Publishing Holdings Limited Partnership
175 Fifth Avenue, New York, NY 10010
mackids.com
First published in 2016 by Penmanship Books, Brooklyn, NY
All rights reserved

Library of Congress Control Number: 2017944500
ISBN 978-1-250-17372-0

Our books may be purchased in bulk for promotional, educational, or business use. Please contact your
local bookseller or the Macmillan Corporate and Premium Sales Department at (800) 221-7945 ext. 5442
or by e-mail at MacmillanSpecialMarkets@macmillan.com.

First Roaring Brook Press edition, 2018
Art direction by Jonathan Key
Book design by Christina Dacanay
Printed in China by RR Donnelley Asia Printing Solutions Ltd., Dongguan City, Guangdong Province

10 9 8 7 6 5 4 3 2

THIS BOOK IS FOR YOU.

BLACK GIRL
THEY SAY YOU AIN'T 'POSED TO BE HERE

YOU AIN'T 'POSED TO
WEAR RED LIPSTICK

YOU AIN'T 'POSED TO
WEAR HIGH HEELS

YOU AIN'T 'POSED TO
SMILE IN PUBLIC

YOU AIN'T 'POSED TO
SMILE NOWHERE, GIRL

YOU AIN'T 'POSED TO   BE MORE THAN A GIRLFRIEND

YOU AIN'T 'POSED TO   GET MARRIED

YOU AIN'T 'POSED TO WANT NO DREAM   THAT BIG

YOU AIN'T 'POSED TO DREAM AT ALL
YOU AIN'T 'POSED TO DO
          NOTHING BUT CARRY BABIES

AND CARRY A NATION—

BUT NEVER AN OPINION

YOU AIN'T SUPPOSED
TO HAVE NOTHING TO SAY
UNLESS
IT'S A JOKE

BECAUSE YOU
AIN'T SUPPOSED TO
LOVE
YOURSELF
BLACK GIRL

YOU AIN'T
SUPPOSED
TO FIND
NOTHING WORTH
SAVING IN ALL
THAT BROWN

BLACK GIRL,
YOU AIN'T SUPPOSED TO
LOVE YOUR MIND
YOU AIN'T SUPPOSED TO LOVE
YOU AIN'T SUPPOSED TO
BE LOVED UP ON

YOU SUPPOSED TO POP OUT BABIES AND HIDE THE STRETCH MARKS

YOU SUPPOSED TO BE STILL

SO STILL THEY THINK
YOU STATUE
SO STILL THEY THINK
YOU CHALKED OUTLINE
SO STILL THEY KEEP
THINKING YOU STONE

UNTIL YOU LOOK
MORE MEDUSA
THAN VIOLA DAVIS

UNTIL YOU SOUND
MORE SHENAYNAY
THAN KERRY WASHINGTON

UNTIL YOU MORE
SIDE EYE
THAN MICHELLE OBAMA
ON A TUESDAY

BUT YOU TELL THEM
YOU ARE MORE THAN
A HOT COMB AND
A WASH 'N' SET

YOU ARE
KUNTA KINTE'S KIN

YOU ARE A
BLACK GIRL
WORTH
REMEMBERING . . .

AND YOU ARE A THREAT KNOWING YOURSELF
YOU ARE A THREAT LOVING YOURSELF
YOU ARE A THREAT LOVING YOUR KIN
YOU ARE A THREAT LOVING YOUR CHILDREN

YOU BLACK GiRL
YOU
YOU BLACK GiRL
YOU BLACK GiRL WONDER
YOU BLACK
YOU BLACK
YOU

MAGIC!

BLACK GIRL FLYY . . .

BRILLIANCE

GIRL SHINE!

GIRL BLOOM!

BLACK GIRL BLACK GIRL

AND YOU TURNING
INTO A BEAUTIFUL
BLACK WOMAN RIGHT
BEFORE OUR EYES

ACKNOWLEDGMENTS

Thank you Falu, for the inspiration in rhythm + spirit.

Thank you to BukBuk ladies: Falu, Eboni + Whitney,
for always being the blackest, most shiniest
magicians.

Thank you Steve Goldbloom + team, for showcasing
this poem on PBS's *Brief but Spectacular* series.

Thank you YCA + Kevin Coval, for the space to share
this poem in its infancy.

Thank you mother, grandmothers, aunties, nieces +
cousins, for a ready example.

Thank you daughter, for the courage and
unconditional love.

Thank you J, for keeping this magic safe.

ROLL CALL

Roll Call is an act of naming the people who brought you into the room. Roll Call is an act of taking up space.

With guidance from the women poets before me, specifically Sonia Sanchez, I offer this roll call. I call forward the names of those who have opened the door for women like me.

This Roll Call is to pay homage to those that make room for us at the table, or nod to us during conversation to ensure that black girls' voices are heard everywhere. The names at the beginning and end of this book are the names that allowed this #BlackGirlMagic to exist.

JOSEPHINE JOY JUDY JUNE JURNEE KAMILAH
KATHERINE KATHLEEN KATY KELIS KERRY
KHADIJA KIA KIM KIMBERELY KRISTA LADAN
LATIFAH LAUREN LEAH LECONTE LENA LESLIE
LIRIS LOLA LUCILLE LYNNE LYRAE LYTE
MAHLANEY MAKAIYA MARIE MARILYN
MARITA MARJORIE MARY MEESHA MELISSA
MENDI MIA MICHELLE MILAN MISSY MONA
MONICA MONIE MORGAN NABILA NADIA
NAFEESA NATASHA NATTY NIA NICOLE NIKKI
NIKKY NILE NTOZAKE OCTAVIA OPAL OPRAH
PAM PATRICIA PENNY PHAEDRA PHYLICIA
PHILLIS PHYLLIS QUEEN RACHEL RACHEL ELIZA